It's Showtime!

Contents   **Page**

written by Diana Burslem

An audience watching a play being performed on stage may not know how many people have worked hard to prepare the show. The group of actors called the cast present the story with the help of the back-stage crew, all busy with their own special tasks behind the scenes. The person in charge is the producer or director, who plans and manages all stages of the production.

Choosing the play

To begin, the producer chooses the type of play and finds a script. There could be music, jokes, dances and songs in the production. Some plays are called "pantomimes", which tell a story with mimed actions, tricks and funny expressions, usually to entertain children.

Next, the producer of the play needs to select the cast – the group of actors who suit the roles. These actors are usually found among the members of a drama club, or by advertising and auditioning.

Auditions

Advertisements for auditions can often be seen on billboards or in newspapers. These notices invite hopeful actors to apply for a role in a new play.

At the auditions, there are lots of people of different ages, all hoping to be chosen for a part. Each person has a turn to read a short script to the director, who listens and observes, taking notes.

TING
1007

Selection success

Before long, the successful actors get the good news that they have been selected. They are given the date and time to attend the first rehearsal, where they will:

- meet the cast and crew
- get a copy of the script
- be given the details of their roles

The production is on its way!

The first rehearsal is just a "walk-through". All the actors read from their scripts and move around the stage in the way the director tells them.

At the next rehearsal everyone must try to say their lines. If they forget, a helper called a "prompt" reminds them from the wings (the hidden sides of the stage). The reminder is called a stage-whisper because it is just loud enough for the actor to hear, but doesn't reach the audience.

With practice at each rehearsal, movements and expressions get better, and all the actors begin to know their cues – that is when they should come on stage and where they should move.

Costumes and props

Costumes are important to make the characters seem real. A crew member in charge of costumes arranges fittings for suitable clothes, wigs, jewellery, hats and shoes. There is advice about stage make-up and hairstyles, too.

"Props" are arranged: this term is short for properties, the items used on the stage, like furniture, books or phones. There might even be a bicycle, a bowl of fruit or a parrot in a cage!

Setting the scene

On Dress Rehearsal night (the night before the real performance), the theater looks quite different. The stage is brightly lit and music is softly playing. A backstage crew has constructed the "set", with large painted scenes forming a suitable background to the stage. An outdoor scene may show a lake, rocks and trees with birds. Indoor scenes might have doors, furniture, curtains and pictures on walls.

All the members of the cast look different too, dressed in their costumes, wearing their make-up and waiting backstage.

When the director says "Curtain Up", the play begins. The small audience includes family and friends, sitting at the front of the theater. At the end of the performance, the audience claps loudly and sometimes people call out "Bravo!"
Later the director tells the cast how to make a few small changes for the real performance the next night: Opening Night.

After the director announces the play to the "Full House"
audience, the curtain rises to show colourful scenery. The actors
take their cues and play their roles. The audience claps as the
final curtain comes down on a successful First Night performance.

Future on the stage

But a play is not just a one-off performance. It takes many weeks of preparation and teamwork to bring it all together, then it runs for a short season. Famous actors often begin their careers with parts in small productions in their home towns.

It's a good way to start learning the skills of acting and of producing a play.